GRAPHIC EXPEDITIONS

Escape from POMPEII

An *Isabel Soto* HISTORY ADVENTURE

Terry Collins

illustrated by Cynthia Martin and Barbara Schulz

Raintree

www.raintreepublishers.co.uk
Visit our website to find out
more information about
Raintree books.

To order:
☎ Phone 0845 6044371
🖨 Fax +44 (0) 1865 312263
✉ Email myorders@raintreepublishers.co.uk

Customers from outside the UK please telephone +44 1865 312262

Raintree is an imprint of Capstone Global Library Limited, a company incorporated in England
and Wales having its registered office at 7 Pilgrim Street, London EC4V 6LB
Registered company number: 6695882

British Library Cataloguing in Publication Data
Collins, Terry – Escape from Pompeii: an Isabel Soto history investigation
A full catalogue record for this book is available from the British Library.

ISBN 978 1 406 21812 1 (hardback)
15 14 13 12 11
10 9 8 7 6 5 4 3 2 1

Designer: Alison Thiele
Cover artists: Tod Smith
Colourist: Michael Kelleher
Media researcher: Wanda Winch
Editors: Aaron Sautter, Marissa Bolte, and Diyan Leake
Originated by Capstone Global Library Ltd
Printed and bound in China by South China Printing Company Limited

Disclaimer
All the Internet addresses (URLs) given in this book were valid at the time of going to press.
However, due to the dynamic nature of the Internet, some addresses may have changed, or
sites may have changed or ceased to exist since publication. While the publisher regrets any
inconvenience this may cause readers, no responsibility for any such changes can be accepted
by the publisher.

...a Belova, 7; Shutterstock/Andrea Danti, 23;
...i, 14; Wikipedia/John Reinhardt, B24 tailgunner,

...en Ping Hung (framed edge design); mmmm (world
...stract lines design); Najin (old parchment design)

CONTENTS

I'm Antonio Giordano. I work here at the Pompeii ruins. I'm showing Maura around. Would you like to join us?

Gladly! I'd love to explore one of the world's most famous archaeological sites.

These ruins are so quiet. It's hard to believe that Pompeii was once a busy city filled with people.

Yes. That all ended when Mount Vesuvius erupted on 24 August in the year AD 79.

ACTIVE OR NOT?

Mount Vesuvius was last active in 1944. Although it has not erupted for more than 60 years, the volcano is not dormant. Scientists believe the volcano will erupt again in the future.

9

In 1864, archaeologist Giuseppe Fiorelli noticed some strange shapes while excavating the ruins at Pompeii.

He thought the shapes looked like people. He decided that bodies must have been buried inside the hardened ash.

As the bodies decayed, a cavity was left inside the hardened ash. Fiorelli poured plaster into this space and allowed it to harden.

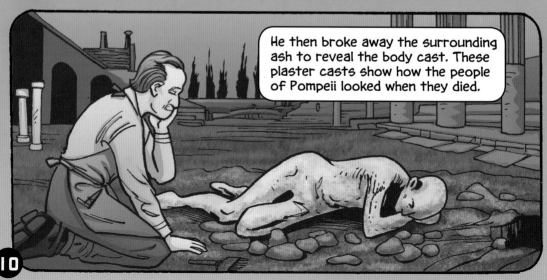

He then broke away the surrounding ash to reveal the body cast. These plaster casts show how the people of Pompeii looked when they died.

POMPEIAN GRAFFITI

The people of Pompeii wrote many kinds of messages to each other on the city walls. They wrote love letters, political ads, angry notes, and funny messages. This early graffiti gives archaeologists a better understanding of how the ancient Pompeians lived.

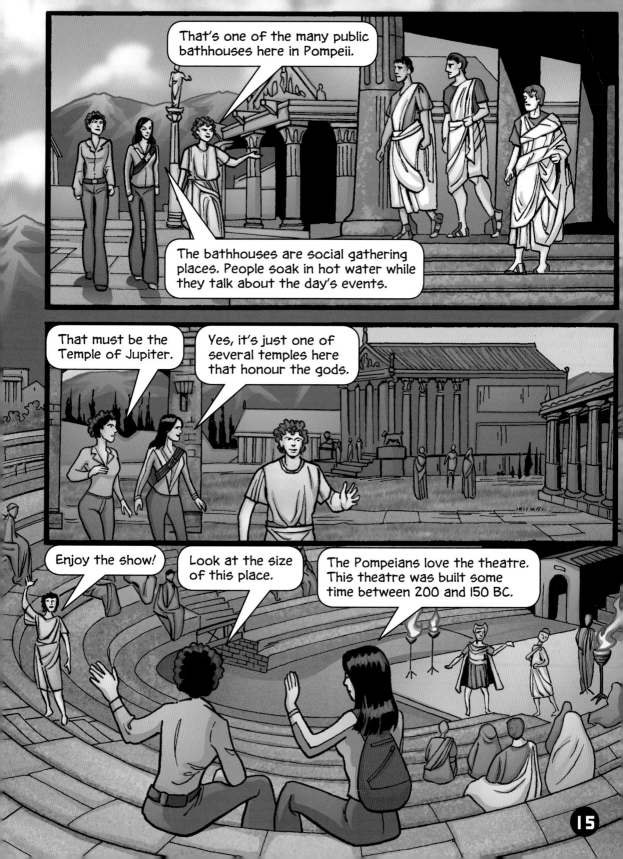

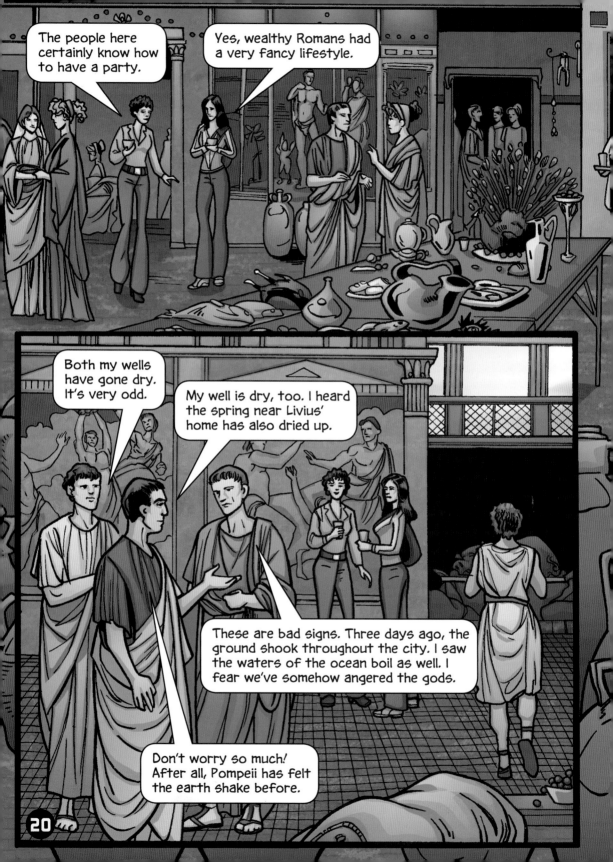

TERRIBLE TREMORS

Several strong tremors served as early warning signs before Mount Vesuvius erupted. While some people in Pompeii chose to ignore the signs, most decided to flee the city until things calmed down. Only a few thousand people were in Pompeii when Mount Vesuvius erupted.

KRAKADOOOOMM!!

THE ERUPTION

The eruption lasted for more than 24 hours. A cloud of hot ash, rocks, and gas, called a pyroclastic surge, came down around midnight. That first surge covered the city with a metre, or 3 feet, of pumice. Eleven more surges completely buried Pompeii.

POMPEII

- During the height of Pompeii's success, the town had 33 bakeries, 130 taverns and snack shops, and 39 wool-processing plants. Many Romans travelled to Pompeii as a holiday spot.

- Pompeii had two theatres used for plays, music, and poetry readings. There was also a large arena used for gladiator contests, which drew thousands of cheering fans.

- The volcanic eruption that destroyed Pompeii is well known from an eyewitness account. Pliny the Younger, a Roman writer, saw the cloud rising from Mount Vesuvius. He wrote two letters full of information from those who had escaped Pompeii. His uncle, Pliny the Elder, died after he went to watch the eruption.

- Pompeii was not the only city buried by Vesuvius. The towns of Herculaneum and Stabiae were also destroyed in the eruption.

- The uncovering of Pompeii first began in 1748. These early digs were destructive. Treasure hunters stole many coins, statues, artwork, and other rare relics. Finally, in 1860, Giuseppe Fiorelli was put in charge and a more careful excavation was begun.

- Since Pompeii was first buried in AD 79, Mount Vesuvius has erupted 80 times. The last major eruption occurred in 1944.

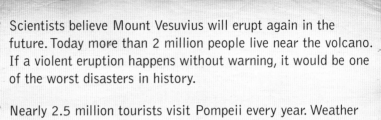

Scientists believe Mount Vesuvius will erupt again in the future. Today more than 2 million people live near the volcano. If a violent eruption happens without warning, it would be one of the worst disasters in history.

Nearly 2.5 million tourists visit Pompeii every year. Weather and heavy tourism have caused the ancient city to begin to crumble. Artwork on the walls has also faded badly. In 2008, the Italian government declared a state of emergency to help restore and preserve the ancient ruins at Pompeii.

MORE ABOUT

Isabel Soto

NAME: Isabel "Izzy" Soto
INTERESTS: People and places
BUILD: Athletic **HAIR:** Dark Brown
EYES: Brown **HEIGHT:** 1.70 m

WISP: The Worldwide Inter-dimensional Space/Time Portal developed by Max Axiom at Axiom Laboratory.

BACKSTORY: Isabel "Izzy" Soto caught the humanities bug as a little girl. Every night, her grandfather told her about his adventures exploring ancient ruins in South America. He believed people can learn a lot from other cultures and places.

Izzy's interest in cultures followed her through school and beyond. She studied history and geography. On one research trip, she discovered an ancient stone with mysterious energy. Izzy took the stone to Super Scientist Max Axiom, who determined that the stone's energy cuts across space and time. Harnessing the power of the stone, he built a device called the WISP. It opens windows to any place and any time. Although she must not use the WISP to change history, Izzy now explores events wherever and whenever they happen, solving a few mysteries along the way.

GLOSSARY

archaeologist scientist who studies how people lived in the past

cast model of an object in plaster. Casts show details of the original object.

cavity hole or hollow space

dormant not active. Dormant volcanoes have not erupted for many years.

excavate dig in the earth

gladiator slave in ancient Rome who fought against other gladiators or fierce animals to entertain the public

graffiti pictures drawn or words written on the walls of buildings or other surfaces

preserve protect something so it stays in its original form

pumice a light, greyish volcanic rock

pyroclastic surge cloud of hot ash, rocks, and gas

relic something that has survived from the past

ruins remains of a building or other things that have fallen down or been destroyed

tremor shaking or trembling movement

tribute gifts given to the gods to show respect

villa large, fancy house, especially one in the country

FIND OUT MORE

Books

The Ancient Romans (History Opens Windows), Jane Shuter (Heinemann Library, 2007)

The Ancient Romans (Understanding People in the Past), Rosemary Rees (Heinemann Library, 2007)

Pompeii, Anna Claybourne and Katie Daynes (Usborne, 2006)

The Rotten Romans (Horrible Histories), Terry Deary (Scholastic, 2007)

Internet sites

www.bbc.co.uk/schools/primaryhistory/romans
Click on the links on this website to find out more about ancient Rome.

news.bbc.co.uk/cbbcnews/hi/find_out/guides/tech/volcanoes/
newsid_1768000/1768595.stm
Learn all about different types of volcano on this website. You can find out what makes them erupt and how scientists can tell whether an eruption is coming.

INDEX